Cats in Disguise

A Costumed Feline Coloring Book
by Hannah Complin

Copyright © 2018 Hannah Complin
All rights reserved.
ISBN:1723448982
ISBN-13: 978-1723448980

In Memory Of

Vyvian Taylor
who loved cats.

Todd Lowe
who loved to laugh.

Many Thanks To

Cable Complin
Kim Shaffer
Kerry Ince
Kendis Cox
Emily Blanche
Amanda Herrera
Laura Finstrom
Mary Moreno
Erica Tan
& the work fam
Thank you for your support!

Contents

1. Lord Cattington takes his catnip from a pipe in his study.

2. Bob is an avid bird watcher who enjoys long walks to the litter box. He donates to PBS regularly.

3. Amelia Aircat likes to chatter on the radio, and at birds.

4. Vyvian the flapper cat is having a great time at Mr. Catsby's party.

5. Brisco is hoping catnip is allowed into Comic-Con.

6. Catherine Kittenworth uses her fan to signal when she wants you to pet her or leave her alone. The signals are identical.

7. "Hold the boat now, tuna man, sir... Put the fishes onto to my plaaaaate..."

8. Shakespeare's cat, Ralph, loved writing because he got to play with a quill.

9. "If I fits, I sits." - Descartes' cat, Mittens.

10. Princess Ripley let down her hair. The prince just played with it.

11. Cookie sales are up this year because of Dolly Catkinson's can-do attitude.

12. Professor Felinicus is inventing a serum that repels dogs.

13. "I swear by my pretty floral bonnet: I will end you." - Captain Tightpants

14. Read 'em and weep. Sailor Rowdy has a full mouse!

15. Major Tom Cat's protein pills are tuna flavored.

16. Ruth Bader Catberg believes access to wet food should be a feline right.

17. This iconic photo of Siggi was taken on the "Scratch Outside the Scratching Post" tour, 1979.

18. Captain Wylie will brave the unknown terrors of hostile planets in search of his nemesis, the elusive Glowing Red Dot.

19. Why is the rum gone? The cat knocked it over. Captain Floofbeard's map leads to "treasure" that nobody wants to find.

20. A witch's familiar, or a witch in cat form? You decide.

When cats throw a costume party, they go all out...

MEET THE CATS

Almost every cat in this coloring book is based on a real cat. Or of course, you can color any of these portraits to look like your cat! That is what makes coloring so much fun.

Cat Models

1. Buddy likes to bask in sunny spots on the floor and contently drools in his owners' arms.
2. Bob is a rescued manx Bengal/American Bobtail mix. He plays fetch.
3. Bug is a cute little tabby with huge green eyes. The dog is afraid of her.
4. Pollywog is a sassy little daddy's girl who doesn't play around if another cat tries to steal her food.
5. Brisco is a 20 lb. grey stray tabby who broke into our house and refused to leave. He loves cuddles.
6. Taisie lives for treats and hot summer days lounging out on the catio.
7. Jack is a tuxedo cat who was once a shy boy and has now blossomed into a total lovebug.
8. Smalls is a 10 year old floof who loves snuggles and his spring toys. He lives in Seattle with his mom.
9. Diesel is a Maine Coon mix who enjoys laying in the sun and rolling around on his dad's dirty socks.
10. Ripley is a feisty little cat princess that doesn't take any crap.
11. Darla chatters at birds who visit the fountain and flirts with solicitors who come to the front door.
12. Renzo is a pro at sneaking kibble from the other cats' bowls and wakes his mom up with kisses.
13. Calera enjoys singing the song of her people in the middle of the night.
14. Rowdy is a grey tabby who lives in Minnesota and is a great brother to his pet siblings.
15. Nike was the world's friendliest lizard killer. RIP
16. Wendy bird and her human live in Orange County, working for the betterment of cats everywhere.
17. Siggi is an imaginary Sphinx. Her guitar sound is heavily influenced by The Stooges.
18. Wylie is a big friendly long haired kitty who lives by the beach in San Diego with his mom.
19. Keefer has one eye in real life. He catches bugs mid-air better than his two-eyed kitty counterparts.
20. Rosetta is a tortoiseshell cat with a heart of gold and a taste for adventure.

ABOUT THE ARTIST

"I like to make things that make people laugh and I like to make people think in a different way. I want to learn to do both through my work."

Hannah Complin's illustration career began in kindergarten, when she discovered that if she drew the Ninja Turtles, other kids would give her quarters for her drawings. She has been creating things for fun and money ever since.

She attended private painting lessons as a teen, and put those lessons to use in college as a theater design major with an emphasis on scenic design and makeup special effects.

She painted throughout school, creating rich, bright and often humorous watercolor pet portraits. She continued to paint realistic watercolors after becoming an instructor at Orange County School of the Arts where she taught for 8 years, and also began to draw fantasy, sci-fi, and sometimes comedic ink illustrations.

She lives in Portland, Oregon with her husband, 2 cats Bug and Brisco, and a Corgi named Sonja.

www.hannahcomplin.com
Instagram: @hannahcomplinart
Etsy: www.etsy.com/shop/HannahComplinArt

PLEASE PARTICIPATE!

CAT MODEL CALL

Do you think your kitty would be a good model for more Cats in Disguise coloring pages? Post your cats on instagram with #instacatsindisguise for a chance to be drawn and featured.

SHOW OFF YOUR COLORING

Do you love coloring and want to show Hannah your finished page from the book? Please post a picture on instagram with the hashtag #complincoloring.

WAYS TO HELP HOMELESS ANIMALS

1. Donate and volunteer at local no-kill shelters.
2. When possible, adopt at-risk animals from kill shelters.
3. Take part in your local trap-neuter-release stray cat colony programs
4. Help people find lost pets.
5. Microchip and spay or neuter your animals.
6. Foster homeless animals, etc... there are many ways to help!

WAYS TO SUPPORT INDEPENDENT ARTISTS

1. Buy our stuff.
2. Don't steal our stuff or use our work without our permission please.
3. Come to our shows.
4. Order custom stuff from us.
5. Tell other people about how and where you bought our stuff and how great it is. Have favorite artists. Be enthusiastic about the arts, and share it with your friends and family.
6. Follow us on social media and participate kindly on artist pages.
7. We are hard-working, skilled professionals. Pay us fairly and treat us with respect, and you will get fantastic results.
8. Do your gift shopping with independent artists and craftspeople. We make all kinds of stuff of typically far higher quality than mass-produced items.
9. Give money to street artists when you see them.
10. Take lessons and learn an art, or put your kids in private art lessons from a local artist.
11. Go to museums and take your kids.
12. Be open to and respectful of art made by people who are nothing like you.
13. If a piece of art disturbs you, think about why.
14. Remember that art is subjective. Something that isn't your cup of tea isn't "bad", it's just different.
15. Take an art history course.

HAVE FUN COLORING & ROCK ON!

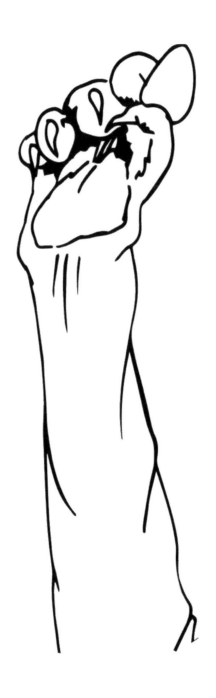